Weather and Erosion

Torrey Maloof

Published by Pearson Education Limited, 80 Strand, London, WC2R 0RL.

www.pearsonschools.co.uk

This edition is published by arrangement with Teacher Created Materials, Inc. for sale solely in the UK, Australia and New Zealand.

© 2015 Teacher Created Materials, Inc.

Text by Torrey Maloof

22 21 20 19 18
10 9 8 7 6 5 4 3 2 1

British Library Cataloguing in Publication Data
A catalogue record for this book is available from the British Library

ISBN 978 0 435 19484 0

Printed in China by Golden Cup

Acknowledgements
We would like to thank the following schools for their invaluable help in the development and trialling of the Bug Club resources: Bishop Road Primary School, Bristol; Blackhorse Primary School, Bristol; Hollingwood Primary School, West Yorkshire; Kingswood Parks Primary, Hull; Langdale CE Primary School, Ambleside; Pickering Infant School, Pickering; The Royal School, Wolverhampton; St Thomas More's Catholic Primary School, Hampshire; West Park Primary School, Wolverhampton.

The author and publisher would like to thank the following individuals and organisations for permission to reproduce photographs and illustrations:
Photographs
(Key: b-bottom; c-centre; l-left; r-right; t-top; bck-background)
Cover Front: Shutterstock: Viktor Kovalenko, Back: **123rf:** Daniel Kaesler, Suppakij1017 b.
Alamy Stock Photo: Morley Read 23, **Getty Images:** Fstop123/ iStock / Getty Images Plus **Science source:** SPL C010/6367 12, CHARLES WINTERS 20l, CHARLES WINTERS 20r, GEORG GERSTER 25t, Andreiuc88 3bck, Joe Belanger 3, Jessica R. McNair 4, TTstudio 4-5bck, Platslee 5, Pigl3t 6-7 bck, Andreiuc88 7t, Alexlukin 9, ESB Professional 10b, Ancher 13bck, JOSE RAMIRO LAGUNA 13, Seth Lang 14, Nullplus 14-15bck, Steve Allen 15, Tooykrub 16-17bck, Jorge Moro 16b, Sevenke 18, Coatesy 19bck, Maxim ibragimov 19, Nagel Photography 21, Lexaarts 22-23, Dima_Rogozhin 24-25bck, Joseph Sohm 25b, Milos Stojanovic 24b, Bobkeenan Photography 26-27bck, StevanZZ 26, Paul Murtagh 27, Jorge Moro 30-31,7b, , 1lt Bobkeenan Photography 31. Baldyrgan, **123rf:** epicstockmedia 10-11 bck.s4sanchita 8-9bck
All illustrations: Teacher Created Materials(TCM).

Note from the publisher
Pearson has robust editorial processes, including answer and fact checks, to ensure the accuracy of the content in this publication, and every effort is made to ensure this publication is free of errors. We are, however, only human, and occasionally errors do occur. Pearson is not liable for any misunderstandings that arise as a result of errors in this publication, but it is our priority to ensure that the content is accurate. If you spot an error, please do contact us at resourcescorrections@pearson.com so we can make sure it is corrected.

Contents

Ever-changing Earth. 4

Wind, Water and More 6

People Play a Part. 22

Seeing Is Believing 26

Let's Try It!. 28

Glossary. 30

Index. 31

Your Turn! 32

Ever-changing Earth

Mountains, rivers and hills may look as though they don't change very much but really, they never stop changing! Over long periods of time, rivers bend and change shape. Cliffs slowly wear away, and even high mountains get broken down over the years.

These changes can be caused by the wind, or by running water. Ice can cause these changes and so can heat from the sun. Even people play a part. Earth's surface has changed a lot over the years and continues to do so.

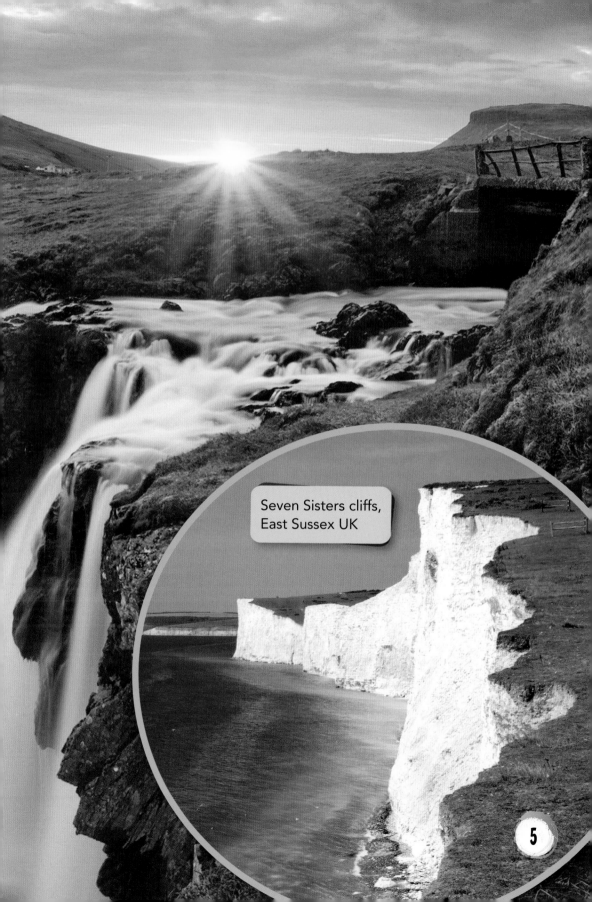

Seven Sisters cliffs,
East Sussex UK

Wind, Water and More

Imagine a fierce storm, with wild wind and pouring rain. What do you think rain and wind do to Earth's surface? They change it! The wind can loosen small bits of dirt and dust from rocks. Drip by drip, rain can wear down rocks and soil. This process is called **weathering**.

a snowstorm

rain

A tornado is a rotating cloud, a whirlwind, that has winds that can reach nearly 480 kilometres per hour – that's faster than high-speed trains can go.

Over time, wind and rain wear down Earth's surface. They break it into small pieces. These pieces are called **sediment**. Wind and water then move the sediment, and carry it away. This is called **erosion**. Weathering and erosion can happen at the same time. They work together to change Earth's surface.

Weathering and erosion are changing this mountainside.

Small rocks, such as these, are easily carried away by this river.

Wild waters

Sediment can blow into streams and rivers. It moves with the water on its way to the ocean. Over a long period of time, rivers carrying sediment can carve into hills or cut into mountains. This is how valleys are made.

Canyons are made in a similar way. A canyon is a deep, steep-sided valley. The Colorado River carved the massive Grand Canyon in Arizona, USA. The Grand Canyon is 446 kilometres long and 2.6 kilometres deep. It took millions of years for the river to carve out this huge canyon.

The Colorado River flows through the Grand Canyon.

the Grand Canyon
near Kwagunt Rapid

This rock shattered as ice froze in its cracks.

Freezing and melting

Sometimes, water turns to ice. This can cause weathering too. Water can run into cracks in rocks. If the air is cold enough, the water will freeze. It turns to ice and expands, or gets bigger. When this happens, the ice makes the cracks in the rocks get wider. It can even split rocks.

Later, if the air gets warmer, the ice in the cracks will melt. It will turn back into water. When this happens, erosion begins. The water from the melted ice carries away tiny pieces of the rock.

As ice melts, the water washes away the cracked bits of rock.

A glacier is a very large mass of ice and snow. It moves slowly down a slope. As it moves, the ice cuts into nearby rocks. Over time, the glacier melts. The water from the melted glacier carves out large valleys.

One such valley is called Yosemite Valley in California, USA. A very long time ago, there were glaciers in Yosemite. As these glaciers moved and melted, they helped to turn Yosemite into the amazing, craggy place it is today.

Yosemite Valley

Sunny California

It's often hot and sunny in California. It's hard to imagine it covered in ice, but millions of years ago, it was!

Yosemite Valley might have been carved by a glacier like this one.

Rhone Glacier, Switzerland

Scorching sun and savage seas

As well as rain, wind and ice, the sun can also change Earth's surface. The sun heats up rocks, and the heat makes the rocks expand. Then, as the air cools, the rocks contract, which means they shrink.

When this happens over and over again, the rocks get very weak. After a while, they begin to crack. They eventually break apart into tiny pieces. Then the erosion process begins and the wind or rain carries away the pieces of rock.

The sun's heat causes large cracks in some rocks.

Over the years, the savage waves of the Southern Ocean as well as wild wind and rain have eroded the Twelve Apostles. These are a group of limestone rock stacks off the coast of Victoria, Australia.

Only the toughest of the rock stacks remain. The shape of these will change and they will become much smaller over time.

Although these rock stacks are called the Twelve Apostles, there are only eight of them.

Plants and animals

Plants also cause weathering. Sometimes, soil builds up in the cracks of a rock. A seed may find its way into that soil. Then a plant will grow in the middle of the crack. As it grows, the plant's roots make the crack get wider and break apart the rock.

Animals can break apart rocks too. Some live underground. They break rocks apart as they move through the soil. Others break rocks above ground. They crush them by running or walking on them.

This plant will slowly break apart the rock as it grows.

Badgers have strong legs and sharp claws. These help them dig burrows and find food underground. Their digging can cause damage to the environment.

Harsh chemicals

Chemicals also wear away Earth's surface. There are gases, such as oxygen, in the air and in the soil. New chemicals can form when these gases mix with water. Some of these new chemicals are acids which can dissolve rocks. This means the acid mixes with the rock and the rock becomes part of the liquid acid. In this way, the rock wears away.

Limestone is a type of rock that acid can dissolve quickly. Acid can make huge cracks in the rock too. It can even make caves!

Acid dissolves limestone.

Cool caves

There are more than 110 limestone caves in Carlsbad in New Mexico, USA. You can walk through them.

Factories can pollute the air.

People Play a Part

People do not cause weathering, but they do speed it up! One way they do this is by **polluting** the air. Cars release unsafe gases. So do factories. These gases make **acid rain** and acid rain eats away at the Earth's surface.

Landslides

When plants and trees are removed, rocks and soil can suddenly slide down a hill. This is called a "landslide".

a landslide in Ecuador

People speed up erosion too, by cutting down forests. The roots of trees help hold soil in place. When the trees are cut down, the soil washes and blows away faster so nothing can grow.

People can stop this damage by erosion control. One way to do this is to build structures that hold soil and rocks in place. Gabions can be used to hold soil in place. These are baskets made of wire, and filled with rocks.

Another way to prevent erosion is to plant trees and plants along shorelines. The roots of these plants help keep soil in place, and they also help protect the shoreline from big waves and storms.

These gabions help hold the soil in place.

These fields have been planted in a way that keeps the soil in place and makes a fancy pattern.

The roots of this plant will help hold the soil in place.

Seeing Is Believing

Whether it's caused by wind, water, ice or sun, or by chemicals or plants, erosion changes Earth. It also creates some amazing sights! Weathering and erosion have made some of the most scenic places in the world – from creepy caves and wonderful waterfalls to crazy cliffs and amazing arches. You really have to see them to believe them!

Over time, water has eroded the cliff to make this arch in Normandy, France.

Victoria Falls, Zimbabwe, is eroding the land around it.

Let's Try It!

What happens when land erodes? Try it for yourself!

What you need

- cardboard
- soil
- drinking straw, cut in half
- polystyrene or cardboard cup
- modelling clay
- sharp pencil
- water

What to do

1 Use the pencil to make a hole in the side of the cup near the bottom. Place the straw in the hole. Use the modelling clay to seal the hole.

2 Place the cardboard on the ground. Raise one end of the cardboard by placing soil under the edge. Cover the cardboard with a thin layer of soil.

3 Place your finger over the end of the straw and fill the cup with water.

4 Hold the cup over the raised end of the cardboard. Then remove your finger. What happened to the soil?

29

Glossary

acid rain – rain that contains dangerous chemicals caused by smoke from factories, power plants and cars

chemical – any substance formed when two or more other substances act upon one another

erosion – movement of weathered rock and sediment

polluting – making dirty and unsafe

sediment – very small pieces of rock, such as sand, gravel and dust

valleys – areas of low land between hills or mountains

weathering – slow breakdown of rock and soil

acid rain, 22

animals, 18, 32

caves, 20, 21, 26

chemicals, 20, 21, 26

erosion control, 24

glaciers, 14–15

ice, 4, 12, 13, 14, 26

plants, 18–19, 23, 24–25,
   26, 32

polluting, 22

seas, 4, 17

sediment, 8, 9

sun, 4, 16, 26

wind, 4, 6–7, 8, 16–17, 26

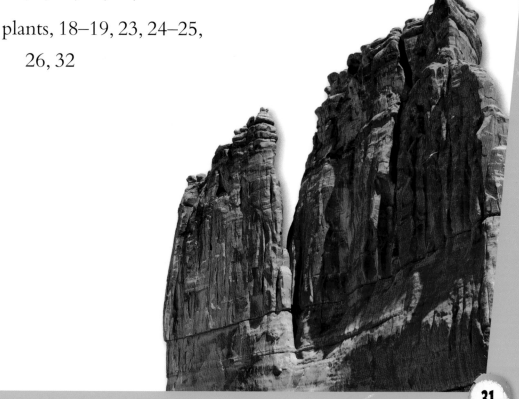

Your Turn!

On the hunt

The effects of weathering and erosion can be seen in many places. You might see cracks in rocks or even valleys carved by water. Go on a weathering and erosion hunt in your playground. Look for signs that wind, water, plants or animals have changed the land.